About the authors

Scilla Elworthy has been awarded the Niwano
Peace Prize from Japan, and been nominated for the
Nobel Peace Prize three times. She specialises in the
effectiveness of conflict prevention and methods
of resolution, and advises political and military
policy-makers. She is founder of the Oxford
Research Group and Peace Direct.

Gabrielle Rifkind is a group analyst, psychotherapist
and specialist in conflict resolution. She is founder of
the Middle East Policy Initiative Forum, and human
security consultant to the Oxford Research Group.

The authors have requested that all royalties from this publication
be paid equally to the following two charities:

Oxford Research Group which works for non-violent positive change
in international security – through research, analysis and dialogue,
focusing on the Middle East, Energy Security, WMDs, and the 'War
on Terror'.
51 Plantation Road,
Oxford, OX2 6JE, UK
Tel: +44 (0)1865 242819 Fax: +44 (0)1865 794652
www.oxfordresearchgroup.org.uk
Registered Charity No: 299436

Peace Direct which funds, promotes and learns from grassroots
peacebuilding in conflict areas, giving everyone an opportunity to do
something practical for peace.
Development House,
56-64 Leonard Street,
London EC2A 4JX, UK
Tel: +44 (0)20 7549 0285 Fax: +44 (0)20 7549 0286
www.peacedirect.org
Registered Charity No: 327947

About Demos This book is published in association with Demos. Demos
is the think tank for everyday democracy. It believes everyone should be
able to make personal choices in their daily lives that contribute to the
common good. Its aim is to put this democratic idea into practice by
working with organisations in ways that make them more effective and
legitimate. Demos focuses on six areas: public services; science and
technology; cities and public space; people and communities; arts and
culture; and global security.
Magdalen House,
136 Tooley Street,
London SE1 2TU, UK
Switchboard: 020 7367 4200 Fax: 020 7367 4201
Email: hello@demos.co.uk Website: www.demos.co.uk

MAKING
TERRORISM
HISTORY

Scilla Elworthy

Gabrielle Rifkind

RIDER

London · Sydney · Auckland · Johannesburg

First published by Demos in 2005 as *Hearts and Minds*.

This revised edition published in 2006 by Rider,
an imprint of Ebury Publishing, Random House,
20 Vauxhall Bridge Road, London SW1V 2SA
www.randomhouse.co.uk

Random House Australia (Pty) Limited
20 Alfred Street, Milsons Point, Sydney,
New South Wales 2061, Australia

Random House New Zealand Limited
18 Poland Road, Glenfield,
Auckland 10, New Zealand

Random House South Africa (Pty) Limited
Corner Boundary Road & Carse O'Gowrie,
Houghton, 2198, South Africa

The Random House Group Limited Reg. No. 954009

Papers used by Rider are natural, recyclable products made from wood
grown in sustainable forests.

Printed by Bookmarque Ltd, Croydon, Surrey

A CIP catalogue record for this book is available from the British Library

ISBN 1846040477 (before Jan 2007)
ISBN 9781846040474

CONTENTS

Acknowledgements

Making Terrorism History is dedicated to Dr Amal Malachi, Iraqi judge and member of the Advisory Committee for Iraqi Women, who joined us at the Amman Roundtable on Human Security in May 2004. She was assassinated in Baghdad in November 2004.

Several individuals made significant contributions to this publication. Rachel Briggs at Demos fostered the idea from the beginning, and Tom Bentley edited the text with great insight. Francis Wilson, Professor of Economics at Cape Town University, gave invaluable help in restructuring it, and Alistair Crooke acts as a living embodiment of the ideas it contains. Professor John Sloboda offered useful material, and Professor Jake Chapman gave critical feedback. Refqa Abu Remaileh skilfully researched the details, Paul Vernon created the graphics, and Johnny Levy patiently supported the process. The determination of Judith Kendra enabled the publication of this new Random House edition, the text of which has been adapted with the skilled help of Bob Davenport. We greatly value all these contributions, and offer our thanks.

Scilla Elworthy
Gabrielle Rifkind

1 INTRODUCTION

Terrorism and political violence have assumed a new profile around the world. Resolving intractable conflicts, especially when some of those involved in them are not acting on behalf of states, has become an even more urgent task since the September 11 attacks and the subsequent invasions of Afghanistan and Iraq.

To achieve peace and security, we now need strategies to combat the use of terror in political and territorial conflicts. But too often this terror is exacerbated – indeed sometimes even triggered – by the actions of governments, both democratic and non-democratic. In this turbulent world, many of the old methods of dealing with conflict seem to be unable to deal with the new realities. Force of arms is not sufficient to establish peaceful order. Military victory is not enough to prevent future violence. Whether we are considering Iraq, al-Qaeda, Chechnya or the Middle East, it is clear that simply trying to hit back and to destroy the 'enemy', the 'terrorists' or the political opponents provides only short-term solutions.

In fact the evidence suggests that such strategies serve only to increase both the level of violence and the yawning chasm between the two sides. The vast superiority in military and economic power of states – American, British, Russian, Israeli – is unable to subdue opponents and bring peace. New thinking and new approaches are needed.

We argue that such strategies will never be successful unless they address the full range of factors that fuel cycles of violence and influence the use of terror. These include the economic, social and cultural context in which violence is sustained. Perhaps even more important, they also include the emotional and psychological effects of violence and humiliation – factors often missing from traditional approaches to counter-terrorism, and especially the 'war on terror'.

Much more is known about how to reduce and prevent violence than our current public debate about terrorism acknowledges. A careful analysis of the root causes of political violence reveals the persistent influence of powerlessness, exclusion, trauma and humiliation, and knowledge of this could usefully inform and influence the development of new security measures. These will be effective to the extent that they are based on principles of non-violence, mutual respect and dialogue, and involve neutral third parties as necessary.

The need for armed intervention and the consistent threat of it may never be eliminated from the way the world is governed. But minimising the use and costs of such intervention is a realistic goal, which all of us have a moral responsibility to pursue.

In *Making Terrorism History* we suggest a different approach to violent conflicts, prioritising the human factor that is often neglected in such situations. We then propose proven practical steps that can – and should – be taken in a wide range of contexts, including Iraq, Israel–Palestine, and also our own towns and cities. In chapter 7 ('What can be done?') we set out a range of measures to resolve and prevent conflict without the use of force. Some of these measures need to be taken at the international level, some at the local level. There are also many initiatives that we can – and perhaps must – take in our own communities to encourage a new society built on understanding, respect and dialogue (see pp. 85–9). The aim is not just to seek immediate resolutions to armed conflict, but also to address and prevent the conditions in which it can be triggered.

Terrorism never entirely can be made history, but how we tackle it will determine whether we exacerbate the problem. Understanding the psychological and emotional causes of political violence is often dismissed as, at best, a nice extra, or, at worst, a harmful distraction from our real world goals. We argue that, rather than being peripheral, the need for a sense of human security must be the starting point of all approaches to terror, political violence and insurgency. This is the only route to lasting peace, and we *all* have a part to play.

2

THE LINKS BETWEEN TRAUMA AND FUNDAMENTALISM

Iraq and the Israeli–Palestinian conflict provide us with timely case studies of the effects of conflict and political violence. They help to demonstrate not just how violent conflict is prolonged through cycles of trauma and retaliation, but also how armed intervention designed to end conflict can often have the effect of stimulating more violence.

To understand why this is, and to understand how such conflicts can fuel fundamentalism, we must look at the psychological effects of these kinds of violence.

IRAQ: THE ROLE OF HUMILIATION, POWERLESSNESS AND DEHUMANISATION

Saddam Hussein's regime established a deep sense of powerlessness among the Iraqi people during years of threat, dehumanisation and fear. Since the fall of the regime it has been compounded by the humiliation resulting from the invasion and the failures of subsequent attempts at reconstruction. That a significant number of the population feel humiliated and dehumanised has become a recruiting agent for terror organisations, and this will continue if ways are not found to address the alienation that ordinary Iraqi citizens experience. The Iraqi people need to have a personal investment in their communities and a sense of hope for the future, yet the trauma they have experienced stands in the way of that. Until this is addressed, progress will be halting and the cycles of violence (see chapter 5) will continue.

When foreign military personnel humiliate men, attack women, children and old people, arrest people arbitrarily, destroy property, and restrict freedom of movement, they provide a painful reminder of the powerlessness felt under Saddam. What is required is precisely the opposite, namely respect. This is not to excuse or condone political violence, however, but to acknowledge that only an understanding of what is really required can lead to interventions capable of dealing effectively with such violence.

Alistair Crooke, an intelligence officer and former security adviser to the EU, with decades of experience in the Middle East, reported from the bombing of Falluja as follows:

> *If you haven't experienced it you can have no idea what it feels like being subjected to bombing of this kind. The houses being destroyed had nothing to do with resistance fighters, who were in any case*

*sleeping in alleyways. Drones going over, utter
powerlessness, helicopter gunships playing cat and
mouse with those they know they can and will kill.
Because bombs were attached to doorbells, the US
troops killed the first person they saw as a matter of
course. This kind of trauma generates intense
hostility. Even if you are an observer, you can't trust
your emotions for a few days.[1]*

FALLUJA

It takes little to squander goodwill in areas of conflict.
Falluja is a prime example of this:

1. Falluja was not hostile to American-led efforts to
remove Saddam from power. Fallujans defied Saddam's
rule during his last years in power, and he was angered
in 1998 when local imams refused to hail him in their
Friday sermons. Many were imprisoned, and the city
was punished. This was certainly not pro-Saddam
territory.

2. In April 2003, before any conflict had erupted in
Falluja, US soldiers opened fire on a demonstration
against the military occupation in a primary school,
killing eighteen people. Until then, not a single bullet
had been fired at US soldiers in Falluja or any of the
cities north of Baghdad.

3. On 31 March 2004 there was the horrifying killing of four American contractors. After the killing of the contractors, the US Marine Corps general persuaded a former soldier from Falluja to engage with the local power structures to set up a local police force. Washington discovered this, and disowned the process. The general was then replaced by another from Baghdad, who both was unknown in Falluja and insisted that US soldiers paraded in the street. He lost credibility, and American policy shifted from one of accommodation to one of threat.

4. The US military then unleashed firepower in urban areas. AC150 warplanes dropped 500-lb bombs, while helicopter gunships fired into densely populated areas. More than 700 people were killed. After the huge numbers of casualties, US forces agreed to withdraw to the outskirts, and the city then became a stronghold for insurgents. The overwhelming use of military firepower increased the rage and potential for political insurgency in Falluja, and is one of the causes of the political problems now present.

5. In November 2004 the US forces and Iraqi allies launched Operation Phantom Fury. The aim was to storm the city and eliminate the insurgents. Falluja's main hospital was seized by US troops in the first days of the siege, in order to control information about the

number of civilian casualties. The other clinic was hit twice by US missiles, and all its medicine and equipment was destroyed. The two ambulances that came to help the wounded were shot at and destroyed by the US troops. After the first siege of Falluja in April 2004, 2,500 people from the tribes joined the resistance; after November those joining numbered 25–30,000. [2]

WHAT COULD HAVE BEEN DONE DIFFERENTLY?

How authority is established in the early days of a conflict is of overwhelming importance, and it may be useful to compare the different rules of engagement of the American forces in the Sunni centre of the country and of the British troops in the Shiite south:

- British troops were allowed to open fire only when attacked, and then to use minimum force directed only at identified targets.
- The British army's response to challenges in its area of control was to establish relationships in the local community, to build communication and confidence. This required a high level of visibility, contact in the street, wearing berets and not helmets, sitting on carpets drinking coffee with local leaders, so the population gain a sense of the soldiers being there to protect them.
- The American reaction to the killings in Falluja did not carry such restrictions of proportional response

or focus on relationship-building. Instead there has been a tendency to elevate the requirements of protecting US forces above those of winning 'hearts and minds'.

It is essential that any response carries a sense of proportionality and restraint. Using heavy firepower in response to the killing of the contractors served only to stimulate the violence and to alienate large sections of the community.

At moments of provocation, a deep sense of fear is stimulated – especially in the case of the US marines, when all their training in containment has been challenged. The natural response to humiliation is a desire for some kind of revenge or retribution. But, at pivotal moments in any conflict, the desire to use overwhelming force needs to be measured against the potential to provoke more violence. It takes enormous self-restraint and wisdom to pause and think of non-violent responses to acts of provocation. However, to seek revenge will only unleash a further cycle of violence. Mature democracies need to find ways to be reflective and contain the violence in moments of fear.

Interventions also need to differentiate between innocent civilians and political insurgents. Otherwise, moderate voices are alienated, thus stimulating the very political extremism that causes anxiety to the West.

WHAT WOULD HAVE CONTAINED THE VIOLENCE AT SUCH FRAGILE MOMENTS?

- A more contained response in Falluja could have served to weaken the case of the insurgents and to keep public opinion on the US side. Lt Gen. James Conway of the US Marine Corps, who led the first major assault on Falluja in April 2004, initially opposed the attack, preferring other methods for pacifying the town. Looking back, he says, 'When we were told to attack Falluja, I think we certainly increased the level of animosity that existed.' [3]

- The steady use of counter-insurgency techniques – such as clearing neighbourhoods in search of potential suicide bombers and smuggled weapons – is more effective when local leaders are consulted about how it should be managed. However, this depends on having established prior contact, employing Arab speakers, and showing respect for the culture and traditions of the country.

- Had the Americans been committed not to 'victory' in Falluja but rather to an isolation strategy and the arresting of insurgent groups, then they might well have not inflamed the local community. An approach using a human-security force comprising trained civilians alongside military personnel, as proposed in chapter 7 (see p. 74), could have done much to contain the violence.

Lessons can perhaps be learned from the experience of the Battle of Algiers, where the French were victorious but at the cost of 1 million casualties. Ron Dudai and Daphna Baram argue that 'victory in the Battle of Algiers did not make occupation any more sustainable. It did, however, scar the French collective consciousness for generations.' They emphasise that 'the price for ruthless violence is exacted from the occupier and the occupied alike.'[4] No matter what the French did militarily, the war dragged on. The French in Algeria, like the Americans in Vietnam, were unable to transform military successes into political victory. Without a political solution and the support of the majority Muslim population, French forces remained isolated in a hostile sea.

The kind of analysis outlined above may help to explain why hostility to occupying troops remains so great in Iraq. But it also points to one of the most powerful ways in which fundamentalist movements can be unintentionally strengthened by repeated humiliation.

In cultures where there have been endless cycles of violence, communities become cumulatively traumatised. It then becomes difficult to enter into the mind of the other, and this in turn makes it hard to build any concern for or interest in the other, or any level of trust – the necessary preconditions for dialogue. This leaves both parties in the position of victim. The culture of perpetual victimhood distorts values, and erodes the vital feedback mechanisms of self-criticism, robbing communities of their most valuable asset, the questioning mind.

STABILITY THROUGH FUNDAMENTALISM

We suggest that there is a direct link between trauma and fundamentalism. Many of the families who identify with fundamentalist groups like Hamas will have experienced their own family trauma or witnessed some deep humiliation or violence inflicted on someone close to them. This is compounded by living in an uncertain, chaotic world in which there is no sense of control and no ability to have any influence. In this situation, fundamentalism offers two things which could give the impression of safety. First is the offer of welfare provision, which cannot be overestimated in terms of providing a material safety net. This shows people that the fundamentalist group is taking care of their best interests and is of benign intent. Second, the presenting of a firm philosophy – albeit extreme in its content – gives the impression of certainty in an uncertain world.

The importance of routine and ritual deserves recognition. If you live in a very uncertain world with a potentially high level of chaos and very little security, external structures such as praying five times a day give a sense of familiarity and safety. Moreover, a strong sense of community and belonging is particularly important when one has very little control over most aspects of one's life. So, for example, if you live in a refugee camp or suffer the indignities of occupation where you feel very little control, to identify with strict codes of practice might offer emotional relief. Members of fundamentalist groups have described themselves as having been hot-headed and frustrated, desperately searching for ways to channel their rage. Prayer, fasting and a belief system constituting a complete way of life offer security and a sense of equilibrium that was previously absent.

In the West, young Muslim men can find themselves torn between the material pleasures of their wider society – such as drink, drugs and sex – and the more puritanical aspects of their parental influences. This can be exacerbated if they have travelled back to their parents' homeland. For example, one of the suicide bombers who attacked London on 7 July 2005, Hasib Hussain, had been sent to a fundamentalist religious school in Lahore for some discipline, as his father thought that Hasib's adolescent behaviour was out of control.

It is now estimated that there are around 3,000 British-born Muslims in the UK who have passed through jihadist training camps abroad. In these camps the Koran is taught as a set of eternal truths, with little reference to its historical context, and the concept of a fairer Islamic society in the form of a caliphate (an Islamic state with Sharia law) becomes a political aspiration that justifies the use of violence to challenge the dominance of Western values. The sense of brotherhood at the camp, and the all-embracing ideology instilled in them, serve as a powerful contrast to the sense of alienation and disaffection these young people may feel back home. Such experiences 'can then make them see the wider British society as shallow and materialistic, reinforcing an "enclave mentality"'. [5]

If you live in a very fragile environment, there is enormous psychological safety in having a clear idea of right and wrong. But this can bring a psychic need for rigid structures and a calcified view of human behaviour. In these conditions the potential to dehumanise the enemy increases, with the loss of the ability to regard them as real people with feelings and ordinary needs. Lost is the recognition of the subtle complexities of human behaviour, of people's propensity for both good and bad. Instead, attitudes that stimulate acute political violence become more entrenched.

OBSERVING CULTURAL SENSITIVITIES

Key to restoring a sense of stability in Iraq is the work already under way to re-establish law enforcement, to retrain and reconstruct the judiciary, and to police the streets. Coalition forces must be fully briefed on how they can not only minimise insult to Iraqis, but actively show respect for the culture and customs of the country. British forces in the South tried to set an example of how to communicate with Iraqis, but more formal training could be provided for all occupation forces. Handbooks do exist to prepare soldiers on the ground for making contact with the local community and to be culturally sensitive when communicating. But such handbooks are of little value unless they are used in training groups in which soldiers can become more aware of their own responses and increase their awareness of communication and some of the assumptions they make when relating to a different culture. It became increasingly clear that, with some notable exceptions, the US military lacked the ability to innovate and think creatively in Iraq. They had been ill-prepared for Arab culture, with its tribal complexities, and had no training in managing the deep rage which was generated by what Iraqis experienced as American disrespect and insensitivity.

No American soldiers had received any but the most rudimentary instruction in the Arabic language or in Iraqi culture. Outspoken army reformer Col. Douglas A. Macgregor, appraising the US military's dilemma in Iraq, said:

> *Most of the generals and politicians did not think through the consequences of compelling American soldiers with no knowledge of Arabic or Arab culture to implement intrusive measures inside an Islamic society. We arrested people in front of their families, dragging them away in handcuffs with bags over their heads, and then provided no information to the families of those we incarcerated. In the end, our soldiers killed, maimed and incarcerated thousands of Arabs, 90 percent of whom were not the enemy. But they are now.* [6]

The American forces in Iraq are perhaps the most isolated occupation force in history: they cannot go out to local bars to relax, and there is no place off their base where they can safely go without body armour in the presence of locals. Every encounter is potentially hostile. [7]

There are deep-seated human-security problems in Iraq that cannot be addressed by any military force. In July 2004, for example, a British Iraqi reported from Kirkuk, 'There are literally hundreds and thousands of conspiracies and rumours in Kirkuk; no one knows the truth of anything, there is utter chaos and people are utterly lost.'[8] His conclusion – similar to that of other humanitarian workers in Iraq – was that a 'bottom-up' policy to instil a sense of human security is needed.

THE VALUE OF LISTENING

This would mean listening in detail to what people on the ground want and need, and providing resources to support them in developing the kinds of community groups, women's organisations, faith-based organisations, professional associations, trade unions, self-help groups, social movements, business associations, advocacy groups and other organisations that constitute a civil society – perhaps incorporating the experience of those who have faced similar problems in Eastern Europe and the Balkans. Mary Kaldor, Professor of Global Governance at the London School of Economics, emphasises that 'Today the challenge, closely linked to the question of legitimacy, is to start engaging from the bottom up. You have to start from the needs of the people on the ground and how they perceive the situation.'[9]

In Amman in May 2004 a Roundtable on Human Security in the Middle East was held to begin such a process.[10] The specialists present – with backgrounds in politics, business, the military, academic research and psychology – contributed their experience of civil society and peace-building in the region, in Eastern Europe before the 'Velvet Revolution', and in Northern Ireland, and constructed a plan for a network of civil-society actors in the Middle East.

So, when trying to understand any conflict, it is essential to consider the cumulative effects of trauma and how this affects cycles of violence (see p. 44). Trauma may be likened to an unhealed wound that festers. [11] Unprocessed trauma increases the subjectivity of experiences, so that people are more likely to see themselves as victims. Others are not to be trusted – 'we can only depend on ourselves' – and the level of pain can become such that it is difficult to look outside, to imagine the experience of the other or to empathise. The world becomes organised around a group's own experience.

3
Understanding terrorism: humiliation and revenge in the Middle East

Terrorism is a tactic rather than a definable enemy. There is no finite number of terrorists in the world to be smoked out, imprisoned or killed. Their numbers are controlled instead by the level of anger and hate that drives people to join their ranks. It is that anger and hate which must be addressed.

At present there are two diametrically opposed views about how to manage terrorism. Some believe it has to be wiped out at all costs by declaring a 'war on terror'. Holders of this view dismiss as an illusion the idea that Islamic radical groups, for example, could transform themselves into peaceful political parties, seeing no place for negotiation with those who are responsible for terror. Others believe that those excluded from a peace process will undermine it, and that among those who take up political violence there may lie a country's future leadership, as became apparent in South Africa.

At one level, terrorism can be seen as a highly organised form of intervention. Terrorists strike at symbols of government to force retaliation and hence elicit sympathy, both internationally and within more moderate circles locally. Provoking government crackdowns and repression will stimulate their more passive supporters to identify with terrorist tactics, leaving little space for moderation.

THE LIMITATIONS OF DEFINING TERRORISM

Labelling insurgent organisations with the single definition of 'terrorist' leads to a predominantly military strategy in which those involved are seen and treated as criminals. A military response may reduce the number of attacks in the short term, but will fuel future violence by antagonising the more moderate voices. It ignores the fact that extreme movements emerge out of social, political and psychological injustice and are often supported by local communities. Thus, as Mary Kaldor suggests, 'To use military means against an assortment of criminals and insurgents, is simply to provoke and consolidate support for those groups.' [12]

Among the well-known groups which are widely labelled as terrorist is Hamas, which operates mainly in Gaza. To those outside the Middle East, the ideas and methods of Hamas may seem extreme. But inside the occupied territories, particularly in Gaza, Hamas is seen as close to mainstream. If Hamas is treated as a criminal organisation, a military response may, in the short term, reduce the number of suicide bombings with which it is associated. However, in the long term, such a response will only fuel future political violence and enlist more moderate voices to extremism. The approach taken by Hamas to the problems faced by Palestinians is sufficiently representative of the community (approximately 30 per cent support Hamas) to require that the group be taken seriously. All this has to be seen in the context of the recent elections in Gaza and the West Bank, and Hamas's current pursuit of political legitimacy.

It becomes increasingly important to be able to differentiate between those with whom it is possible to communicate and those hardliners who are not open to any kind of dialogue. In March 2005 the International Crisis Group published a report warning against a 'sledge-hammer approach which refuses to differentiate between modernist and fundamentalist varieties of Islamism'. In adopting such an approach, it commented, 'American and European policy-makers risk provoking one of two equally undesirable outcomes: either encouraging the different strands of Islamic activism to band together in reaction, attenuating differences that might otherwise be fruitfully developed, or causing the non-violent and modernist tendencies to be eclipsed by the jihadis.' [13]

ENGAGING MODERATE VOICES

In the first instance, it is possible to engage the moderate voices in non-governmental organisations and other bodies, in the hope that they may eventually be able to reach those who are unreachable at present. Crooke argues, 'if there is to be any really meaningful dialogue with political Islam, the West needs to accept the role of listening, actively promoting symmetry in dialogue, and being ready to accommodate alternative discourses on the experience of modernity'. [14]

It is tempting to see terrorism as springing from poverty and illiteracy. But, however undesirable these are, they are not the root causes of political violence. Many terrorists are of middle-class or privileged origins and well educated, and those who support them are likely to be more educated than their fellow citizens.[15] Peter Mansfield writes:

> *Islamic activism was the creation not of the poor but of the frustrated middle class . . . it gained a following not in the shanty towns of the North African cities, but on the campuses of universities and technical colleges. Arab students volunteered to fight in the Afghan jihad . . . in the same spirit as their left-wing European counterparts in the 1930s went off to fight in the Spanish Civil War.*[16]

This comparison gives a more accurate impression of the passions behind Islamic activism than analyses based solely on fundamentalism or sexual repression (see pp.38-9): for some young Muslim men, being exposed to satellite images of the ruins of Falluja – transformed into a ghost city, with more than 700 of its inhabitants killed – generates similar feelings to those produced by the bombing of Guernica which led volunteers to fight in Spain. Likewise, the Baader–Meinhof gang members who terrorised Europe in the 1970s were well-educated German students.

Humiliation is one of the principal root causes of terrorism. Harvard scholar Jessica Stern emphasises that this state is extremely important in explaining why terrorists are so successful in recruiting large numbers of young men. There is a powerful correlation between acts of humiliation and the desire to restore honour and pride by using violence. Such actions as Palestinian men being stripped naked in public at checkpoints by Israeli soldiers, restricting freedom of movement, lethal use of military forces by Israelis, house demolitions, confiscation of land, the bulldozing of olive groves, and, more recently, the construction of the 'security fence', however they are understood by those who carry them out, result in an acute loss of dignity and are experienced as humiliation. With such an emotionally, physically and politically intangible force as a driving factor, it becomes clear that terrorism cannot simply be understood by reference to such factors as poverty, political constellations and power struggles, or historical events.

Individuals who have accumulated an unquenchable desire for vengeance may be in no frame of mind to communicate or to end the violence. They may be so angry that their desire for retaliation and revenge (see figure 1 in chapter 5) is greater than their capacity for reason and reflection. Their hatred may be so intense and entrenched that rational argument is impossible. Indeed, they may wish to foreclose all further discourse by becoming suicide bombers, whether as young women walking into a public space with explosives strapped under their clothes in Israel or Chechnya or as young men flying a crowded passenger aeroplane into New York's World Trade Center.

4

THE GROWTH OF
SUICIDE BOMBING

The increasing role of suicide bombers in terrorist attacks is a matter of particular concern to all those seeking to create the conditions for peace. According to Madeleine Bunting, writing in the *Guardian*, we find it difficult to comprehend suicide bombing partly because it is the opposite of how we believe wars are now fought. She writes:

> *The West can only now kill from a distance –*
> *preferably from several thousand feet up in the air or*
> *several hundred kilometres away on an aircraft*
> *carrier. It is the very proximity of these suicide*
> *missions which is so shocking. This kind of intimate*
> *killing is a reversion to pre-industrial warfare – the*
> *kind of brutality seen in the thirty years war, for*
> *example.* [17]

The mechanism of psychological 'distancing' makes it possible for a soldier to fire canisters of buckshot at jeering children in Mosul, Iraq, for example, while explaining, 'It's not good, dude; it could be fatal, but you gotta do it.' [18]

We need to look more closely at the motivations of those who choose to become suicide bombers. It is easy but inaccurate to assume that suicide bombers are poor, uneducated religious fanatics who are emotionally unstable and depressed. That profile simply does not fit the facts. A study conducted by the Pakistani journalist Nasra Hassan suggests that suicide bombers do not come from one particular socioeconomic background. Between 1996 and 1999 Hassan interviewed nearly 150 recruiters and trainers of suicide bombers as well as suicide-mission volunteers. He wrote of his findings that:

> *none of the suicide bombers – they ranged in age from 18 to 38 – conformed to the typical profile of the suicidal personality. None of them were uneducated, desperately poor, simple-minded, or depressed. Many were middle class and held paying jobs. Two were sons of millionaires. They all seemed entirely normal members of their families.*[19]

The important question is not simply how sociopolitical conditions affect motivation, feelings or actions, but how and why they affect different people differently.[20] There are many reasons why people become suicide bombers, and it is not possible to generalise. Each individual will have their own personal reasons for choosing this role. Yet one factor is almost always essential: an organisation behind the bomber – not least to convince the recruit that this is the ultimate sacrifice, and to see that he or she goes through with the act. Looking at suicide bombers' biographies, Werner Bohleber notes that group members are inculcated with a:

> 'shared state of aggressive numbing', an orientation towards the attack ahead, an erasure of all prior scruples, and an extermination of all doubt and any sense of empathy for those who will soon be victims of the attack. This is the submersion into a parallel world from which there is no 'point of return' . . . What is always killed in such acts is one's own weakness, doubts, and conscience, which are projected upon the other. [21]

'Often the decisive part is a written or videoed testimony in which the recruit declares his or her commitment to what they are about to do.' [22] Israeli psychologist Ariel Merari of Tel Aviv University, an analyst of suicide bombing, says that this is the point when a recruit becomes a 'living martyr' and it is then virtually impossible to back out. (Some weeks after the 7 July 2005 attacks Londoners saw the video testimony of Mohammad Sidique Khan, one of the suicide bombers involved – a mentor for disadvantaged children at his local primary school, and ostensibly a pillar of the community.) The video may be seen as part of a process of brainwashing. The very act of making a video becomes a public activity in which a suicide bomber makes a commitment not only to himself but to the group. To then withdraw would be a deep betrayal and humiliation, something he may well feel he cannot live with. The sense of duty to a brotherhood of peers is, many psychologists agree, the single most important reason why otherwise apparently rational people can be persuaded to kill themselves and others.

This would go some way, but not far enough, to explain why seemingly normal young men leading a suburban existence in northern England – 'unremarkable' is how they have been described – launched the 7 July attacks. It was their very 'unremarkableness' that their surrounding communities found unnerving, stimulating the kind of anxiety present when one does not know who one's next-door neighbour is. People began to fear that the presentation of ordinariness was merely a façade. In practice, the emotional process at work in the suicide bombers was one of splitting, in which they presented ordinariness to the outside world, but at the same time were leading a double life. This kind of splitting often involves training and using brainwashing techniques. Parallels may be seen with the training of spies in espionage.

It may be useful to examine what is meant by brainwashing here. It is not some sort of magic, but a secular scientific method that acts on the human brain in order to change belief systems. Central to the process is the need to isolate the individual. In the case of the suicide bombers, this may well have happened in training camps. It also becomes important, when brainwashing, to narrow the 'field of view so that everything becomes interpreted through one ideological lens'.[23] The brainwashed needs to be exposed to repetition as the more familiar the idea the more comfortable he becomes. All this is reinforced by the intensity of the group process, his identification with and sense of belonging within a particular group. The importance of group identification cannot be underestimated as many of the young men who are potential candidates for causes using such methods are often lonely, isolated and alienated in their societies.

With respect to the bombings carried out by these individuals, what has to be considered is whether a particular bombing is viewed by the planners simply as strategic. In the case of the London bombings, those running the organisation behind the bombings may have concluded that the most effective way to influence British opinion against the occupation of Iraq would be to convince Londoners that their lives would not be safe until the troops were withdrawn.

There is an implicit assumption that suicide

bombing is irrational, but there are often strong strategic reasons why this tactic is being used. It could be argued that suicide bombing is the only weapon that Palestinians have against the Israelis and that it has created a balance of terror which has forced the Israelis to negotiate. Alternatively, it can be argued that it draws attention to the extremity of the conflict and increases support for Hamas. Can young men who see themselves as filled with noble ideals not feel, as in earlier wars, that they should sacrifice their lives for their people? Why else did kamikaze pilots commit suicide?

When someone is exposed to traumas and humiliation in a context of social and political violence, they tend to experience these both as an individual and as a member of a group. Thus 'the need for revenge and rectification of the harm done may then not only be personally motivated, but may also gain strength from a need to restore the group's identity and honour'.[24] Wounded by territorial disenfranchisement and ethnic humiliation, terrorists seethe with the desire for vengeance. Added to this is the pent-up sexual frustration which is common in sexually segregated societies.

Many of the suicide bombers are in their late adolescence or early twenties – an age when confusion around identity may produce a crisis about who one is. In such conditions, one is more susceptible to thinking along ideological lines and, potentially, brainwashing.

One stereotypical analysis is that many young men are facing thwarted lives without sexual pleasure or hope, and to become a suicide bomber may seem to provide a 'magical escape', with the promise of sumptuous erotic pleasure in paradise. But it is much too naive to think that the promise of carnal bliss with seventy-two heavenly virgins would drive young minds to participate in the cult of suicide bombing. Much more likely is a sense of powerlessness, rage, hatred and injustice.

Some may become convinced that they are the vanguard of a revolutionary movement opposed to the decadence of Western culture. They may believe that by striking a dramatic blow at Western values and the Western way of life they can create a different society. As Alistair Crooke has put it, they convince themselves that their violence is part of a global game of psychological chess. The extremity of their views and their murderous tactics put them in a minority, but their sense of alienation and disapproval of the values of the West is shared by a large number of Muslims.

A deeper inquiry is needed into the explosive mix of religious and sexual repression, the accumulation of humiliating experiences and the psychological pay-off for those who become suicide bombers. The young suicide bombers of the second intifada are the children of the generation who experienced the first. They witnessed their parents' profound impotence and humiliation, and chose a more extreme identity in an attempt not to re-create their parents' experiences. The Palestinians felt that they had tried non-violence, and it did not work. They felt abandoned and betrayed both by the Arab world and by the international community. Moreover, in spite of the optimism that the various peace processes may have brought, material conditions have continued to worsen. Continually dashed hopes have built up to create a more deeply ingrained anger and despair. Children at a Palestinian school in Al Khader, south of Bethlehem, were found to be badly affected by the constant violence. One eight-year-old was so traumatised that her hair turned white. Constant fear, speech problems, nightmares and eating disorders are quite commonplace.[25]

Radical ideology alone is not enough to explain the creation of a suicide bomber. Subject to an intensely stifling social milieu, and encouraged by charismatic leaders, the suicide bomber finds violence not only legitimate but also deeply gratifying.

This suggests that the act of suicide bombing is calmly and consciously used as a political instrument and as a *last recourse in trying to resolve past struggles*. It is important to remember that for the first thirty years of their political struggle and desire to bring their political plight to the world stage, the Palestinians did not use suicide bombing.

What happens when a society loses any sense of hope

or investment in the future? When do things become so desperate that a 'dignified' death is preferred over living in shame and humiliation? When this coincides with a situation where daily life is harsh in the extreme – as in Gaza, where it is difficult to find work, receive medical help, or travel from place to place – people become ready to identify with a culture of death rather than life. When people are being killed every day for no apparent reason, life for young people becomes so futile that life after death can seem preferable.

A basic way to reduce suicide bombing would therefore be to introduce systematic efforts to restore a sense of respect, or at the very least to remove daily humiliations such as roadblocks, body searches, night raids on houses, and disrespect of women. A positive development is the recently created 'Machsom [Checkpoint] Watch' movement set up by Israeli citizens. However, the problem remains one of basic injustice, with the result that young Palestinians feel deeply alienated, hopeless, furious and alone in their struggle. Equally, current measures taken by their own government are not making Israelis feel safer.

The same may be true for some Chechens. In an article for the newspaper *Nowaja Gaseta*, Mainat Abdulajewa writes:

Ajsa Gasujewa, twenty-two years old, from Urus-Martan in Chechnya, was the first Chechen suicide killer in 2000. What led the beautiful woman with green eyes into the military headquarters of Urus-Martan with an explosive belt around her body was the loss of sixteen of her closest relatives, killed by Russian military within barely a year of the beginning of the war – among them her husband, two brothers, one sister, several cousins and nephews. Ajsa's husband, who belonged to the rebels, had been wounded and held captive; the same day General Gadschijew, the military commander of Urus-Martan, visited him in the regional hospital. He had no questions for the patient: he stepped forward to him and drilled a bayonet into his chest . . . Thereafter Ajsa had managed twice to speak to him and ask for the release of the bodies of her husband and her brother, but Gadschijew wouldn't give in. During her last visit he promised her, in front of witnesses, to bury her alive if she was to dare again to appear in front of him. Thereafter the woman left her home and wasn't seen for two weeks, until she showed up on the morning of 10 June 2000 in front of the headquarters' gateway.[26]

5

WHY DO PEACE PROCESSES COLLAPSE?

Time and again political leaders try to establish dialogue through 'peace processes'. Often under pressure from outside, they undertake negotiations and in some instances manage to reach an agreement, which is then acclaimed by the media. To widespread astonishment, these carefully crafted agreements then come apart, and violence breaks out again. The whole pack of cards collapses. Why? Moreover, why do 50 per cent of countries emerging from war fall back into war?

The short answer is that unless peace is established at the grass-roots level, unless the tiresome, difficult, unglamorous work of rebuilding people's lives has been done, unless people are in a mood to live with their neighbours, no amount of coercion or shuttle diplomacy at the top will produce a lasting peace.

BREAKING CYCLES OF VIOLENCE

This is because people, as well as communities or nations, get caught up in deadly cycles of violence. These cycles are deadly because they ensure that one conflict leads straight into another, often involving more and more killing. The classic cycle of violence – which has been evident in the Israeli–Palestinian conflict, in central Africa and repeatedly in different regions of former Yugoslavia – has roughly seven stages, as shown in figure 1 below.

Figure 1 shows how the cycle of violence works in the human psyche, at the level of emotions. If conflict resolution is to work, it is at the human level that it must operate, because the origins of the cycle can be dismantled only within the individual human heart and mind.

Figure 1 The cycle of violence

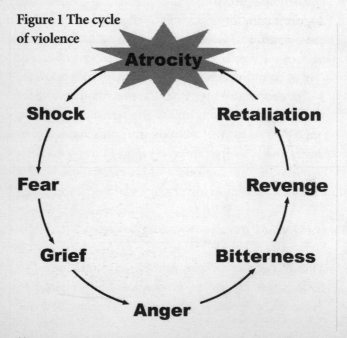

Intervention is needed at the point before anger hardens into bitterness, revenge and retaliation (see figure 2). To be effective it must address the physical, the political and the psychological security of people trapped in violence: all are equally important, and tackling one without the others will be insufficient to break the cycle. In every case, the people involved in situations of violence must be supported in developing their own resources for change.

This is why strategies for building peace must address the physical, psychological and political dimensions of

Figure 2 Point of intervention

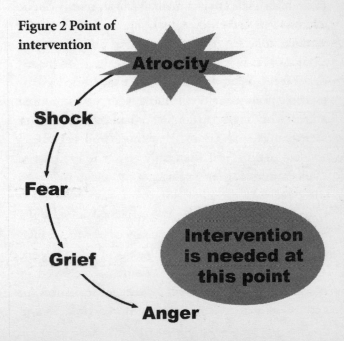

Atrocity

Shock

Fear

Grief

Intervention is needed at this point

Anger

security simultaneously, and seek to combine political negotiation and formal agreements with changes that are evident much closer to everyday life.

PROVIDING PHYSICAL, POLITICAL AND PSYCHOLOGICAL SECURITY

Obviously, the first priority is to provide physical security, so that people feel safe to venture out of their houses. Improved methods of peacekeeping,[27] violence monitoring, disarmament and gun collection can help to establish a safe environment. Political security can be addressed by law enforcement, the establishment of a working judiciary, a free press and in due course free elections. These essential steps have been addressed elsewhere.[28] What has hardly been addressed is the psychological security of those who have endured atrocities or long-term conflict. Whether in a family or society, it is well known that those who have been severely traumatised frequently go on to traumatise others, unless their experience is recognised and addressed.

In South Africa under the apartheid regime, the humiliation and brutality experienced by African men at work has translated into high levels of violence against the next in line – women. Dr Naeemah Abrahams observes: 'One of the consequences of decades of apartheid – state-sponsored violence and reactive community insurrection – is that for many people physical violence has become a first-line strategy for…gaining ascendancy.'[29] A study among working men in Capetown found that 42 per cent of its participants reported physical violence against an intimate partner, and in South Africa as a whole four times as many women as in the US were killed by an intimate partner.[30]

THE PALESTINIAN–ISRAELI CONFLICT

For the Palestinians, there is a profound sense of injustice that goes back to their experience of *Al-Nakba*, which is the Palestinian word for what they regard as their catastrophe, when large numbers of refugees were displaced as a result of the 1948 war. The occupation compounds this injustice, particularly the loss of the home: studies show that among children the worst kind of trauma after losing their mother is losing their home. The resulting vulnerability and insecurity can translate into nihilistic violence. This violence becomes central to the culture, and is passed from one generation to the next.

For the Israelis, part of their society is still traumatised by the impact of the Holocaust, indelibly etched on their political landscape. The death of 6 million Jews represents the terrible period in history when the Jewish people were unable to protect themselves and were unprotected by the rest of the world. The Jewish state, since its founding and during its subsequent evolution, not only has had to defend itself in a hostile environment but has not felt able to rely on anyone else to help protect it. Thus, in certain sections of the community, there is a passionate belief in self-sufficiency, open defiance towards the rest of the world, and a total disregard of outside public opinion.

The following case study illustrates what happens when trust breaks down completely, how incomprehensible the point of view of each side is to the other, the lengths desperate people will go to in order to survive, and the drift from criminality to warfare. It also shows that if the central paradigm for security is viewed solely through the lens of one's own security, and causes a great deal of suffering for the other side, it will only provide short-term protection and is likely, in time, to lead to an acceleration of the conflict.

GAZA: PEOPLE TRAPPED IN VIOLENCE – THE RAFAH WEAPONS-SMUGGLING TUNNELS[31]

The Oslo Accord (1994–5) granted the Palestinian Authority control over most of the Gaza strip. The agreement specified that the Israel Defense Forces (the IDF) would continue to control a narrow strip between the areas under Palestinian control and the border with Egypt, which is called the 'Philadelphi Route'. Israel claimed that Rafah, a refugee camp in this area, had become one of the main pipelines for weapons-smuggling and was the 'oxygen for the intifada'.

Tunnels had been built in residential areas in order to avoid detection. The entrances were usually covered by cement and hidden behind furniture or panelling. The weapons smuggled through these tunnels included RPG rocket-launchers, AK-47 Kalashnikovs, explosives and ammunition. Because of trade restrictions imposed by Israel on Gaza, the tunnels were also used for smuggling cigarettes, car parts, electrical goods, foreign currency, gold, drugs and even caged birds. This smuggling had become one of the main means of making a living in the area. A power struggle developed between different clans over control of the smuggling, involving terror organisation and crime gangs.

Israel's response to uncovering forty-five of these tunnels during the building of the wall along the Philadelphi Route was severe. Israeli helicopters pounded Rafah with missiles and machine guns.

There was growing opposition among the Palestinian civilian population to the tunnel building and weapons-smuggling. This led to demonstrations by residents demanding the securing of tunnels by the Palestinian Authority police force, which conducted a well-publicised operation to expose the tunnels and arrest the smugglers.

Humanising initiatives on Israel's behalf – that is,

asking the Israelis to be more empathic to the suffering of the Palestinians, and thus accept policies based more on the needs of the community – became difficult to envisage in the climate of hate. The situation could be likened to an ugly divorce in which the role of external arbitration and mediation becomes crucial, to allow a period of cooling-off. When trust has broken down, one can no longer rely on the goodwill of both sides. Those deeply involved in the cycles of violence are too caught up in the trauma to move beyond their desire for retribution and think about the long-term needs of both communities.

Most Palestinian people see anything that does not end the Israeli occupation as merely palliative. From their perspective, the political violence will not be reduced until they experience some legitimate participation in the political process and feel that there is a real prospect of statehood. Israel's withdrawal from Gaza will be seen as an honest gesture only if it is part of a wider withdrawal from the West Bank and offers the prospect of a viable contiguous state for the Palestinians.

WHAT CAN BE DONE?

- The demolitions in Rafah have been one of the most divisive issues between Israelis and Palestinians. The Israeli government could reduce the suffering of the Palestinian community by

offering to rebuild their homes or by offering
compensation. If it is unable to do this, it could
hand the role over to a third party. Such actions
would reduce hatred, as people would have a real
prospect of security.

■ Serious economic investment in the Palestinian
territories by the international community would
offer a genuine possibility for economic
development and the move towards self-sufficiency.
Only real possibilities for economic growth will
reduce smuggling. The evident Palestinian
entrepreneurial spirit can only flourish in less
adverse conditions.

■ The use of military strikes may, in the short term,
weaken the enemy and its potential to retaliate, but
it may be provoking a more cataclysmic event from
a more desperate Palestinian population. Military
strikes must therefore be reduced.

■ Israel is reluctant to entertain the thought that
Hamas may be not only the problem but also part
of the solution; however, it may need to recognise
that widening participation to include the voice of
Hamas will be necessary to reduce the violence.

■ The Human Rights Watch report (March 2005)
examined the homes of 16,000 Palestinians in Rafah
that the Israel Defense Forces had destroyed in the
name of stopping weapons-smuggling through
tunnels. After consulting tunnel-engineering

experts, reviewing satellite imagery and conducting extensive field research, Human Rights Watch showed that Israel's legitimate security concern with stopping the weapons-smuggling could be met without this massive home destruction – by using anti-tunnelling technology that has been successfully deployed in the far tougher environments along the Korean demilitarised zone and the US–Mexican border.

- In such intractable situations, finding long-term solutions requires an extended period of recovery for both sides, long after physical safety has been established. This probably needs third-party intervention for peace enforcement, thereby ending the occupation and offering the possibility of strengthening the Palestinian community and reducing the likelihood of political violence. [32]

6

IS NON-VIOLENCE
AN OPTION?

Other peoples besides the Palestinians have been subjected to grave injustice. What has sustained them in the face of this, and what has enabled them to transform it? What about the Tibetans, for example, hundreds of thousands of whom were murdered, tortured or driven out of their homeland? What might the Dalai Lama say to a young Tibetan who wants to blow himself up outside a Chinese military camp in Lhasa?

> *If we use violence in order to reduce disagreements and conflict, then we must expect violence every day. Furthermore, it is actually impossible to eliminate disagreements through violence. Violence only brings even more resentment and dissatisfaction.* [33]

Tibetans have not got their country back yet, but by renouncing violence in this way the Dalai Lama has made the Tibetan cause known and respected worldwide, and has gained the support of most world leaders, Buddhism has become the fourth largest spiritual practice in the world, and there is a growing interest in non-violence across the globe. [34]

TOWARDS PEACEFUL RECONCILIATION

If we want non-violent ways of pursuing political goals to become more widely practised, even in the face of ruthless violence, then we need to understand how military and diplomatic intervention can be informed and accompanied by methods which help to create a real possibility of peaceful reconciliation. This will not happen unless efforts to make and keep peace, develop governance and recover from war are able to address the psychological effects of trauma and humiliation.

There is an urgent need to find a political language that recognises trauma, especially in trying to promote dialogue between groups of people who are not fully rational and objective. To what extent can leaders who have a deeply traumatised history think and act rationally? How far do their experiences affect their political judgement? These questions need to be factored in to make dialogue more effective.

Western democracies often assume that debate needs to be conducted according to rational principles that reflect the values of the West. For example, assumptions are made about secular society which, in the minds of the Western power elites, means democracy, power-sharing and women's rights. In contrast, the experience of secular rule in the Arab world is linked with authoritarianism, whereas Islamic laws of governance include notions of inclusiveness and welfare which were not experienced under secular, authoritarian, regimes. Olivier Roy writes:

> *In the West, secularisation is seen as a prerequisite for democratisation, but in the Middle East it is mostly associated with dictatorship, from the former Shah of Iran to President Ben Ali in Tunisia ... In Muslim countries secularisation has run counter to democratisation, the best example being the cancellation of the Algerian parliamentary elections of 1992 under the pretence that they would have been won by the Islamists.* [35]

The long-term impact of deep shame and humiliation on people's psychological structures, and the consequent effects on political discourse, are frequently underestimated. Where communities have been traumatised, they cannot be expected to conduct dialogues according to Western rules of rational behaviour.

What is needed in such cases is the building of relationships that are sustained and nuanced – the kind of communication where real trust can be built over time, in a climate of respect and open dialogue. It is tough and exacting for the international community to help foster such a deeper level of engagement, and it may appear that there is no room for real dialogue as there is so huge a chasm in thinking. Violence may reflect a deep history of exclusion and injustice, whose wounds are very raw and the resulting hatred very deep. In this state of mind people do not participate in the kind of discourse with which Westerners are familiar. Highly trained and skilled mediators and negotiators are required to engage in this in-depth work.

A new kind of introspection is needed within Western political methodology, not least to allow engagement with groups such as political Islam, whose voices need to be listened to more carefully. To make this dialogue fruitful it may be necessary to examine some of the shortcomings of Western secular liberalism, and how some genuine political values have been subverted in favour of a narcissistic society. Westerners may need to question their beliefs about democracy and freedom, and recognise that many of their values may appear hypocritical and self-serving to the Muslim world.

Islamic communities also need to be self-critical and take responsibility for some of the difficulties they face in their own communities. This requires a shift from a culture of blame to looking at what can be done to prevent the alienation of their young people and what help may be needed to support this.

THE ROLE OF CIVILIANS AND CIVIL SOCIETY

Over ten civilians are killed for every combatant in modern wars,[36] and the same is true for the effects of political violence. Our recommendations in chapter 7 thus emphasise the role that civilians and civil society, as well as governments, can play in minimising political violence. Some of the most effective methods look to ancient (and very modern) traditions of non-violence.

Non-violence is very definitely not passivity: it requires rigorous training and deep conviction. The effect it has on violent, cruel or angry people is more powerful than yet more violence. It affects them at a profound level. Its power is what Martin Luther King taught and used to vast effect in desegregating the deep South. It is what Aung San Suu Kyi used when she walked, unarmed, straight up to the machine guns of Burmese soldiers who had been ordered to shoot the demonstrators she led. It was the power behind the 'Velvet Revolution', which brought down the Iron Curtain. In non-violence you are risking your life (if necessary) so that no one else will be killed, whereas in combat you are risking your life to kill others; and a suicide bomber is deliberately using his or her life to kill others.

Nelson Mandela, who arguably has prevented millions of deaths by averting civil war through dialogue with the De Klerk government, asserted in his trial on terrorist charges before the Pretoria Supreme Court in 1964 that there are situations in which political violence is legitimate.[37] He spoke of a violence that does not lead to loss of human life, and instructed his followers never to plan in advance to injure or kill human beings. Most of the attacks undertaken by the black liberation army of South Africa were on public buildings and strategic targets that symbolised apartheid.

For non-violence to become effective, massive support will be required to make it a household word, to become the natural alternative. Socialising young people to reject violence as a means of problem-solving is key to any sustainable resolution of conflict. This would have to start at the beginning, in families and schools. In Israel, for example, news from the grass roots and the classroom is much more positive than news from political and military leaders.

Non-violent communication training – the brainchild of Marshall Rosenberg – is being used to great effect in Israeli primary schools. In the United States, more than 50,000 schools use a programme on 'Teaching Tolerance'. Children in Boston public schools write their personal stories and read them aloud in class so that they and their classmates can learn to see other people's perspective and develop empathy. If peace proves elusive for today's generation of adults, these programmes inspire hope for the next one. Professor

Michael Nagler reports that teachers and administrators have been surprised to find not only that the programmes 'chill' a lot of the violence in school yards and classrooms, but that a peculiar pattern emerges all across the country: the biggest troublemakers turn out to be the best mediators.[38] Non-violence starts from a positive statement: 'How can I make a creative, constructive long-term impact on the situation I'm in and, ultimately, on the world I'm in?'

7

WHAT CAN BE DONE?

If terrorism is to be contained and its impact on civilian populations reduced, policies for peace and security will need to move on from the existing bias towards military intervention. We are not simply arguing for a more sparing use of military force: we are arguing that armed intervention should be both preceded and followed by a much wider range of strategies designed to address both the causes and effects of violence, as well as to end the immediate manifestations of conflict.

In this chapter we suggest a range of practical steps that can help make terrorism history. We believe they could be used to positive effect in Iraq, Israel and Palestine, and more widely. Their principles should inform both decision-making by governments and the conduct of armed forces and development organisations in conflict situations.

LOCALISED ACTIONS

1. AVOID, WHEREVER POSSIBLE, USING MORE VIOLENCE
Nothing should be done that supports the image of the

terrorist as a heroic warrior defending the interests of the people. Incidents like Abu Ghraib, the killing of innocent civilians in Falluja and the firing of tank shells into the Gaza strip make it easier for militants to legitimate their campaign of violence in the eyes of their own communities, repugnant though it may be to many outsiders.

The main reason for the failure of the Islamic revolution in Algeria and Egypt was that most people wanted to have nothing to do with men who mutilated and maimed innocent people. In the global context that holds true too. It is the moderation and humanity of the vast population of the world of 1.3 billion Muslims . . . that will see us through the darkness that lies ahead and take us toward an end to both terror and the war on it. [39]

2. SHOW RESPECT

Humiliation is a key driver of political violence. Humiliation and degradation are ancient and explosive weapons of war. Conversely, to redress and reduce violence requires soldiers and all those involved in conflict to be systematically trained in the necessity for respect for other cultures. **This means, for the training of all armed forces, not only an awareness of customs and religious sensitivities and learning at least the basics of the language concerned, but also education**

in awareness – understanding **why** respect is so important. The concept is easy to grasp at the personal level: someone who feels deeply insulted by another is hardly likely to behave in a peaceful and cooperative way; whereas, even if there is profound disagreement, differences can often be sorted out if the other speaks in a respectful, non-aggressive manner. What is effective between two people is also effective with groups and between nations. The personal is indeed political.

At key moments, respect can save lives in ways that guns cannot. The US officer who ordered his men to 'take a knee' in an explosive encounter with enraged civilians in Falluja was using not only his initiative but his understanding of the need for respect. Great courage is needed to defuse violent situations in this way.

3. IMPROVE PHYSICAL CONDITIONS

Reduction in political violence is likely to be achieved by a genuine improvement in conditions. **In Iraq and in the occupied territories, this means creating jobs, encouraging rebuilding, providing access to medical help, re-establishing schooling, removing hindrances to trading, encouraging voter registration and a free press, abolishing curfews and roadblocks as soon as possible, and stopping any unnecessary searches or intimidation.**

4. INCLUDE ALL PARTIES IN THE PEACE PROCESS

If a framework for conflict resolution does not recognise the importance of popular support, then any peace deal will be less likely to be sustainable, not least because those excluded from the process will attempt to undermine the agreement. A British intelligence officer with years of experience of the Middle East reports that **intervening governments need to be aware that externally imposed 'top-down' political solutions are unlikely to survive unless they go some way to include those previously excluded, particularly when there is a deep mistrust of the political process.**

Insurgents use violence in an attempt to gain political legitimacy. Giving a voice to insurgents could minimise their desire to create more violence and attack a system that excludes them. However, there is a danger of handing over political power to extremist groups whose use of violence may have become deeply embedded in their actions and risks becoming normalised as a mode of communication. Men of violence are brutalised by their experiences: violence becomes a way of life, and once they have political power it often becomes their tool. There are lessons to be learned from the Irish case, where power given to men of violence resulted in a continuation of the same violence. In such cases, it becomes crucial to find ways to prevent bullying tactics from taking over and to open up conflict-resolving processes to voices that are serious about choosing non-violent options.

In South Africa there are many examples of engaging with the interests of the violent. Although on a small scale, this one, which involves a school in Lavender Hill, a particularly violent township, may be useful. The school was plagued by robberies. The headmaster had tried everything – locking equipment in special storerooms, increased security, alarms – but the thefts went on. So, in desperation, he asked for a meeting with the local gangsters, which was arranged secretly with the help of the clergy. He asked the gangsters what their problem was. No jobs, no money, they replied. He thought for a while and said, 'I haven't got bricks for my building programme. If I were to set up a simple concrete-block-making facility in the school yard, and give you jobs, would you ensure no more crime?' They agreed to his proposal, the deal was done, and from then on the school was fiercely guarded.

5. ENCOURAGE CIVIL SOCIETY, AND CONSULT

A golden rule for effectiveness in policy formulation is to consult with community organisations. Where there are few community organisations, encouraging their growth will prove beneficial. **Social movements such as the Middle East Citizens' Assembly (MECA) are new and need support.** They are modelled on the civil-society initiatives that prepared Eastern Europe for independence from the Soviet Union and played a large part in ensuring that the revolution there was 'velvet' and not bloody. MECA is a participatory organisation to enable people in the region to move from victimhood to being active in society through a sense of shared responsibility. Such organisations will by definition be working at the grass roots, running training courses in non-violence, citizenship, non-governmental organisation and civil society. A good model here would be the initiatives taken by Serbians to rid themselves of the Milosevic regime – in particular by training students to monitor elections, and by the many initiatives to set up a free press and establish the mechanisms of civil society.

In Afghanistan, the Coalition for Peace and Unity (CPAU) organised a consultation for civil-society groups to which they invited the local warlord, who had a private army of 2,000 men. He agreed to attend the first day for reasons of protocol, but stayed the entire week and became deeply engaged with a workshop on dehumanisation. Mohamed Sulciman, chair of CPAU, led the workshop as follows. He drew a diagram of two children born into similar circumstances. He showed child A having a normal, loving upbringing and becoming a doctor. He showed child B losing both his parents in an accident, having to beg on the street to stay alive, being abused, and becoming a thief. 'Who',

MAKING TERRORISM HISTORY

asked Suleiman, 'do we blame? We have to ask why child B became a thief. We also know from experience that he can change.' The warlord became so engrossed with this line of reasoning that he decided against the use of force and went home and dismissed his army.

6. SET UP CENTRES OF LISTENING AND DOCUMENTATION (CLDs)

These would be responsible for a number of activities, including:

- documenting severe abuse and violations of human rights such as vigilante killings, torture, rape, disappeared relatives and unlawful arrest, in order to organise, redress and, ultimately, establish some form of restorative justice
- assessing damage and injury caused by the occupation forces, making restitution, and taking legal and disciplinary action in public
- deep listening. The essential principles to be borne in mind are to listen to what local people express as their needs, to support what they want and feel able to do, and to use the skills already existing on the ground. When large numbers of people have endured horror, it becomes important to create space in which they can humanise their relationships and move beyond demonising the other.[40] Listen carefully to the demands of

66

community leaders, and find out what would be the conditions under which the violence could stop. Are there initiatives within the local communities that could be supported to help manage the violence? Where the voice of violent protest reflects a significant part of the community, find ways to include it in the political process. This was done with spectacular success in South Africa, and has been the key factor in decreasing violence in Northern Ireland.

In the case of Iraq, these functions could have been carried out by the Coalition Provisional Authority and could now be carried out by the Iraqi government in cooperation with the occupation forces and with support from the international community. The concept of CLDs should also be taken into policy planning, for example in the UK Foreign Office Post-Conflict Reconstruction Unit.

7. Trauma counselling

In Croatia, in the midst of the war, a small group of citizens set up the Centre for Peace, Nonviolence and Human Rights in Osijek. It has now grown into one of the largest citizen-led peace-building organisations in the Balkans, with over 300 active members. The Centre sends 'peace teams' to towns and villages to aid the healing of trauma that has left so many people emotionally scarred. In places where Serbs still live, the peace teams have made important progress in reducing the level of animosity and tension between Serbs and Croats, thus reducing the likelihood of violence breaking out anew.[41]

Wars and violence rest on the presumption that those being attacked are not human. Dehumanising the enemy is a defence mechanism that does not allow space for taking responsibility for the consequences of one's own actions. Fear shapes the process and allows it to continue, massively reducing the capacity to think about and engage with the other side. With time, a desire for backlash builds up and can manifest itself through physical action. Thus a balance needs to be struck between self-protection and preserving the humanity and integrity of the other side.

Traumas experienced by victims of atrocity need attention and, if possible, healing. For example, women victims of rape and torture speak repeatedly of the need for psychosocial healing, trauma counselling and support.[42] One way in which this can be provided simply and effectively is through careful listening, whereby an independent witness or witnesses gives the traumatised person their full attention for as long as necessary, allowing them to discharge their fear, grief and anger. This simple technique takes time and care, but done well it prevents anger hardening into bitterness and retaliation. The military needs to consult and work closely with organisations such as the Red Cross, Médecins sans Frontières, and the Medical Foundation for Victims of Torture, to set up trauma-counselling centres.[43]

8. Train and employ a significant number
of women

In development work worldwide it is now commonly accepted that women are effective agents of change. A significant number of women should be trained for the police forces – both for regular duties and to address rising violence against women in public places and in the home.

In Iraq, where women constitute 62 per cent of the adult population and represent a vast currently unused resource for peace-building, this role will require encouragement, support and training by the new Iraqi government. For example, two-thirds of Iraq's teachers are women, but they have yet to receive the funding promised to support their initiatives for post-conflict reconstruction and capacity-building in their organisations. A national education process is needed to inform women of their rights and responsibilities, to raise awareness among men of the value of including women in every walk of life – including politics – and to expand training programmes preparing women to assume key posts.

Connections with women leaders in the West and in other Muslim countries should be supported with funding.

All member countries of the United Nations have signed UN Resolution 1325, which recognises the vital role that women can play in de-escalating violence. **In every region, not just the Middle East, it will prove cost-effective to allocate funding to training women to play an equal part in peace education, conflict prevention, peace negotiations, mediation, and post-conflict reconstruction.** Such formal training helps restrain and influence men of violence.

In Kenya, where inter-tribal killing in the early 1990s had claimed 15,000 lives in Wajir on the border with Somalia, the initiative of a Muslim woman brought together the women of the two tribes to force the men to negotiate. Their commitment was absolute. They said, 'If a member of your family is killed by a member of mine, will you still work with me for peace? If you can't say yes, don't join.' The process was so effective that the Kenyan president gave the initiator an office in his government, to extend the practice to other areas of the country.

The 2004 Amman Roundtable cited the examples of the preponderance of women in building the Helsinki Citizens' Assembly in Eastern Europe, contributing to the non-violence of the 'Velvet Revolution'; the role played by the Women's Peace Party in negotiations for the Good Friday Agreement in Northern Ireland; the initiative of Liberian women to bring about disarmament before elections from 1993 to 1997; the Women's Organisation of Somalia, which emerged in the midst of war to prepare the groundwork for peace, etc.

9. TRAIN SKILLED NEGOTIATORS AND MEDIATORS

In order to build dialogue in areas of conflict, significant numbers of negotiators will need to be trained both at a grass-roots level and in the international community. 'Non-state actors could provide training in conflict resolution to relevant parties including village elders, citizens, politicians, the military and others.'[44] A roster of eminent persons, experts and former military personnel could be created – a group of wise and experienced public figures who wish to use their in-depth skills for mediation.

10. WORK WITH RELIGIOUS LEADERS

In Iraq, various attempts were made to work with imams and sheikhs. However, in many cases the initiatives were stopped by the US authorities before they reached fruition. In other cases, when attempts were made to bring representatives of different belief systems together, a successful outcome was precluded by efforts on the part of Western diplomats to instruct the leaders on what they should do.

In other situations, meetings of religious leaders have helped to resolve conflict, or church organisations have acted as mediators – notably in Nicaragua (1984), Mozambique (1992), Guatemala (1996), Sudan (2001), South Africa (1991), Mali (1996) and Liberia (1999). **In Iraq, in particular, even today, the occupation forces could, if they showed sufficient respect, develop a relationship with religious leaders and support them to play a much greater part in negotiating an end to violence.** For example, in Falluja after the killing of US contractors in March 2004, a negotiating team of sheikhs from Anbar province proposed to the US forces that if they withdrew to their bases, and stayed there, they could guarantee a peaceful situation. This was not accepted or acted on by the US military.

11. BRIDGE-BUILDING

The efficacy of bridge-building between communities fractured by decades of violence became evident in Northern Ireland, where it has been recognised as an essential part of efforts to overcome deeply ingrained community hatred and suspicion, with particular attention being paid to schoolchildren. For example, in the late 1980s and early 1990s 'Education for Mutual Understanding' was established to enable children to learn to respect and value themselves and others, to know about and understand what is shared as well as what is different about their cultural traditions, and to appreciate the benefits of resolving conflict by non-violent means. Such processes could be introduced in Iraq with suitable cultural modifications.

12. EVENTUAL TRUTH AND RECONCILIATION PROCESSES

The lies, suspicion and betrayals that characterise war can fester for decades and erupt in further atrocity if not addressed. This needs to be done in public and in a safe and controlled environment, and one of the most effective methods is a truth and reconciliation commission.[45] To date there have been twenty of these, each building on the lessons of the last, the most well known being held in South Africa from 1995 to 1998. **The British government could take steps to initiate a truth and reconciliation process in Northern Ireland.**

The demands of reconciliation with a view to ensuring a peaceful transition to a democratic society often necessitate postponing or rationing justice for the victims of gross human-rights violations and their families. In place of conventional justice, involving legally sanctioned punishment for crimes committed, efforts are made to expose the egregious acts and systematic violations of the past and to establish accurate and detailed records of them. Debate about the efficacy of truth and reconciliation commissions often revolves around the requirements of expediency and the imperatives of justice and law, but overall such

Figure 3 Transforming
the cycle of violence

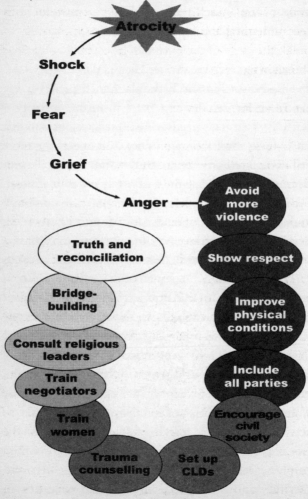

commissions do perform a vital restorative function within transitional democracies, and help to break the cycle of violence. In fact, all of the twelve actions recommended above could be used cumulatively to break the cycle of violence described in chapter 5, as shown in figure 3.

GLOBAL INITIATIVES

1. COMBINE MILITARY AND CIVILIAN PEACE-BUILDING

Policy-makers are beginning to encourage such developments as a combined military and civilian peacekeeping force. Such a force would enable military and non-military capacity to be jointly planned, developed and deployed to the greatest good of the populations concerned. A recent report delivered to European Union defence chief Javier Solana recommends a **Human Security Response Force of 15,000 men and women,** one-third of them civilian. Instead of aiming principally to minimise their own casualties, the aim would be to minimise all casualties.[46] Like police officers and firefighters, these people would be deployed on human-security missions in which they would risk their lives to save others. The principles of service – suggested by Mary Kaldor, convenor of the working group which produced the report – would combine traditional military values like heroism, sacrifice and excellence with civilian qualities of enabling and listening to others. The goal of such a force would be not victory but the cessation of violence, and first and foremost to protect people, calm violence, and establish the rule of law in order to find space for political solutions. In addition, a Human Security Volunteer Service would be made available both for mid-career professionals looking for a career break and for graduating students.[47]

At national and international levels, such an initiative might require accommodations on both sides. **Military planners would need to engage with civilian peaceworkers far earlier and more comprehensively than they might feel comfortable with. Conversely, peaceworkers might have to temper their critical independence with a pragmatic commitment to dependence on, and partial 'inter-operability' with, military forces, particularly in the early stages of deployment.** Such accommodations must be made, to provide the best chance of putting right the mistakes of the past and avoiding further unnecessary bloodshed.

In the United States, in response to the challenge of making peace, a Nonviolent Peaceforce is being formed. This 2,000-member professional paid corps – along with 4,000 reservists, 5,000 volunteers and a research division – will aim to respond wherever there is conflict around the globe. In four years the project, operating from offices in St Paul and San Francisco, has received endorsements from seven Nobel Peace laureates, has established bases in Europe and Asia,[48] and has built up a network of participants and potential volunteers from around the world, emphasising the global South. This new project, if it succeeds, will result in a worldwide peace service capable of intervening in a conflict or incipient conflict more quickly than the UN peacekeeping division and – more importantly – with a different kind of power from that of national militaries. 'While the US government insists there is no alternative to endless war, the Nonviolent Peaceforce is quietly attempting to institutionalise a proven alternative. If it succeeds, the world will have two kinds of standing army to choose from.'[49]

2. THIRD-PARTY INTERVENTION

In deep-rooted conflict, hatred and mistrust are so profound that it is impossible to build either trust or peace until violence has been contained. When atrocities and indiscriminate violence are mutually inflicted, the parties may need to be separated, with the opportunity to cool off until the pain of the trauma is less intense and rational thought is more feasible. There is an important role here for third-party intervention, undertaken by a reliable neutral international body. **It is essential that any form of intervention is not seen as occupation. Critical to this is whether the 'outside' peace enforcers impose their philosophy 'top down' or whether they are prepared to liaise very carefully with**

the people on the ground, paying full attention to what they would see as an improvement in their lives.

In a research monograph published by the Project on Defense Alternatives in May 2005,[50] Carl Conetta outlines how a foreign military presence can be perceived as more or less legitimate despite a popular disposition against occupation. He emphasises that this depends on how the foreign military relate to local authority and to popular needs and aspirations. Using Iraq as a case in point, he lists three sets of issues that are relevant:

- humanitarian needs, post-war reconstruction, and material quality of life
- maintenance of social order and security
- self-determination.

What matters, therefore, is not only whether intervention is undertaken but *how*. Carefully constructed partnerships are needed which are seen as strengthening the work that is already being done in local communities.

Methods that would help foreign military forces to establish better relations with local authorities would include:

- reaching agreement with both parties to send in peace enforcers, to establish a separation zone and police a ceasefire

- establishing some form of trusteeship where governance of an area has broken down, to restore order and basic safety
- ensuring the safety of refugees where necessary
- getting involved in institution-building and the strengthening of civil society
- administering appropriate humanitarian aid – but always working towards greater self-sufficiency for the community
- working with and supporting grass-roots organisations in their work of bridge-building and stabilisation.

3. CUT THE EXPORT OF WEAPONS

Four members of the UN Security Council – France, the Russian Federation, the UK and the US – are responsible for 78 per cent of global exports of conventional weapons.[51] About two-thirds of these exports go to developing countries and regions of conflict. This trade in arms foments violent conflict.[52] It is estimated that up to 90 per cent of all illegal small-arms trade begins with state-sanctioned trade.[53] The economic arguments for arms exports and the rationalisation in terms of the 'need to protect jobs in the arms industry' habitually offered by exporting governments have been comprehensively refuted.[54] **Cutting the export of weapons, on the part of the**

Permanent Members of the Security Council, would send a message of greater integrity to the politically violent, as well as decreasing the availability of the tools of violence.

4. LONG-TERM SUPPORT FOR PEACE PROCESSES

At present, there is no fully effective overarching institution that has the authority to assess when and how intervention in a conflict is appropriate. Intervention is fragmented and often at the instigation of a particular international player, whereas what is needed is a comprehensive, systematic analysis that pays attention to all the conflicts in the world, assessing their needs and the rights and responsibilities for intervention. While in theory the United Nations has the authority to make decisions on intervention, it is often limited by the vested interest of different parties involved, and this leads to a chasm between intention and political will.

An example of this occurred during the Palestinian–Israeli conflict, when in the Camp David process the Clinton and Barak governments were obliged to put pressure on the peace process and speed it up in a way that may have been a critical factor in its collapse. The United Nations is not sufficiently trusted by Israel, and is not seen to be neutral. In addition, there has not been a sustained and committed process that has involved all the different players in an attempt to establish a final agreement.

What is needed is a permanent organisation able to act as a consistent and stable mediator, taking primary responsibility for any peace process throughout its different stages. **A neutral Peace and Security Commission that has the authority to intervene in all areas of conflict with a long-term commitment should be set up for this purpose.** Central to the development of the Commission would be that it is permanent, possibly authorised by the United Nations, but at the same time independent and able to act swiftly without bureaucratic limitations. **Research into the establishment of a Peace and Security Commission could be funded by the Advisory Council for the Human Security Commission.**

The Commission's task would be to engage all the parties at the different levels of political decision-making and civil society as appropriate. It would insist that all those involved in a conflict be participants in the peace process, paying particular attention to those who have been excluded and may have resorted to political violence. Such a process would take as long as necessary, but consistent proactive engagement would be essential in spite of any attempts to derail the process.

In Northern Ireland, Senator George Mitchell's capacity to listen fully ('as long as it takes')[55] to those from all sides has been credited as a key factor in the eventual negotiation of the Good Friday Agreement. Mitchell also observed that a reduction in violence in the context of broad popular support for peace-building is quite different from a reduction in violence enforced against the grain of popular sentiment.

Furthermore, the Commission would be expected to be alert to emerging conflicts and to the role of early intervention. It would be required to track and analyse every conflict consistently, to develop relevant intervention and resolution methods, and to be responsible for providing mediation, dialogue and intervention in peace processes, continuously analysing the effectiveness of different methods and their applicability in specific situations. It would also be charged with convincing governments of the importance of the human-security agenda if they are contemplating military intervention, and would have the responsibility to insist that planning for post-war reconstruction is closely integrated into any military intervention.

Such an institution would need considerable financial resources and to be able to employ those with proven effectiveness in negotiation: former world leaders, military specialists, experts in conflict resolution, and human-security consultants. A substantial body of trained mediators drawn from all religious and cultural backgrounds is required, and it would be important to have an equal balance of men and women. Its methodology could draw on the work of the International Crisis Group, which is an independent, non-profit, multinational organisation with over 100 staff members on five continents, working through field-based analysis and high-level advocacy to prevent and resolve deadly conflict. It could be funded by a tax on currency speculation (such as the Tobin Tax), and be governed by representatives of explicitly neutral countries.

5. ESTABLISH HORIZONTAL NETWORKS TO COMBINE LEGITIMACY AND NEUTRALITY

The demand for political legitimacy – the right to be heard – by those who use violence must be assessed in terms of the extent to which they truly reflect the views of the community they claim to represent. In the Gaza strip, for example, Hamas has the support of 30 per cent of the population and needs to be acknowledged as a serious political voice. People may not like its methods of getting heard, and may even have difficulty with how it wishes to organise society, but in the end real security lies not in military strength but in engaging with those who feel excluded from the political process. In the short term this may reduce the possibility of a Western-style democracy, but the increased possibility of creating a national consensus may be the necessary first step towards a more open society and to stemming the tide of Islamic fundamentalism.

Some people would argue that the legitimacy of NGO representatives is more difficult to confirm than that of national governments, who are at least elected and therefore accountable to their electorates. Others counter this by claiming that the legitimacy of Western governments has been permanently damaged by revelations of mendacity to their electorates concerning the reasons for intervention in Iraq. As for their neutrality in the Middle East, it would be hard to establish or defend claims for this. And their questionable records only emphasise the need for other means of ensuring both legitimacy and neutrality.

A useful model here would be the Helsinki Citizens' Assembly, which built a broad and active constituency – a horizontal network – for its work of democracy-building in Eastern Europe before the fall of the Berlin Wall. Representatives of citizens' organisations, then illegal in the countries of Eastern Europe, met annually during the 1980s, first in Helsinki and then in other capitals, to discuss and decide upon a viable methodology for democratic accountability. This model is to be adapted to the uses of the new Middle East Citizens' Assembly.

Under discussion at the Amman meeting on human security in the Middle East in May 2004 was the question of setting up a **human-security network**, to include representatives of organisations working on aspects of democracy-building, election monitoring, human rights, mediation, protective accompaniment, women's rights, bridge-building, truth and reconciliation, restorative justice, violence monitoring, weapons collection, and education in peace and justice. If such a network were to be adequately funded, from truly neutral sources, it could become the basis for real protection for its members, rather like a trade union. It could eventually build sufficient strength to address some of the other causes of war – especially resource shortages and the profits being made out of war, including traffic in weapons and women.

PERSONAL MEASURES

So far this chapter has discussed organisational initiatives – whether on a localised or a global scale – that we believe can help make terrorism history. However, there are also steps that individuals can take to reduce the tensions on which violence feeds.

After the attacks on New York and Washington in September 2001, the Madrid bombings of March 2004 and the London bombings of July 2005, one of the symptoms of the resulting climate of anxiety was a suspicious and even hostile attitude towards the Muslim community in some quarters. In such circumstances people reduce their contacts with and increase their distance from groups of whom they have become fearful. Yet common sense tells us that to do this runs counter to what is in our best interest. What we need to do is to reduce the space between people and make real contact. This is more likely to create a safer world than distancing ourselves from those whom we imagine we fear. The more contact that any of us have with those who are unfamiliar to us, through race, religion or cultural background, the less likely we are to demonise or stereotype the other. Initiatives to support contact and encourage the building of relationships can make a real difference.

These are examples of what we as ordinary citizens can do to help reduce the level of tension in Western society:

1. **Contact-making:** Whether you are a member of a Western, Muslim or multicultural community, a useful initiative would be to make contact with a neighbour of whatever background and get to know them. Think of small yet important ways in which you can foster a sense of community spirit that includes all members of society.

2. **Anxieties and fears:** If you are sitting on a train and there is a bomb scare, a possible reaction is to withdraw and isolate yourself. In these circumstances, isolating yourself often increases your anxiety and leads to distorting and magnifying fears. It is more helpful to

make contact with other people in this situation, find out how they are, and share your own anxieties.

3. **Multi-faith dialogue:** If you are a member of a religious community, for example, a church, a mosque or a synagogue, you can participate in multi-faith dialogue. This offers the opportunity to form relationships and reduce potential political, cultural and religious misunderstandings between groups.

4. **Schools** can provide an opportunity for engaging and understanding other cultures. Most schools actively encourage this. Parents could also take initiatives to set up projects which involve visiting each other's homes, joining in each other's cultural activities, and potentially bridging the gaps where misunderstandings might occur.

5. **Sporting events** also offer the opportunity to reduce conflict between groups. Israelis and Palestinians have set up their first joint football team. Glasgow Rangers is another example: despite deep traditions of religious hatred, the management of the club has made it clear that any sectarian behaviour is unacceptable. The experience of joint participation humanises the opponents and reduces levels of misunderstanding.

6. **Public spaces** offer opportunities to interact with

groups whom we think we fear, while at the same time being sensitive and avoiding intrusion. Examples of this can be an interchange at the local market, or a sensitive conversation with the local greengrocer or at the local community playground.

7. **Local radio:** Phone your local radio station and ask them to host a regular phone-in programme on community understanding. This could be anchored by community leaders – especially women – of all faiths, and each day could tackle a range of subjects, from 'What part does religious belief play in your politics?' to 'How does it feel to be a young Asian man travelling with a rucksack?'

8. **Weblogs:** There is scope for setting up a weblog as a way of communicating between groups who historically have wanted to have very little contact and between whom there has been suspicion. It could offer an opportunity to work on understanding different points of view and different ways of seeing.

9. **Violence:** If engaging with protest groups who support violence, you could try to encourage them towards civil disobedience or other forms of non-violent protest. Lying down in the street could have a more powerful effect than detonating a bomb.

10. **Support non-violence:** In every conflict there are people brave enough to take the difficult path of non-violence. You can support them by joining Peace Direct tel: 0845 4569714 (inside the UK), or email info@peacedirect.org

11. **Local office:** Elect people to positions of local authority who are committed to active understanding between communities – people who are personally warm and not trapped in one set of ideas. Stand for office yourself!

If such contacts are to be valuable and enhance relationships, two ingredients become crucial here:

■ the capacity to listen carefully and try to understand why people are seeing things differently, rather than reacting or defending
■ the ability to put oneself in the other person's shoes and imagine why they think as they do.

If you are bold enough to take such initiatives, you can expect to be ridiculed, but the most important thing is to keep doing it.

8

MAKING TERRORISM HISTORY

The practical suggestions we made in chapter 7 are not 'easy'. They require maturity, and intense training, as if to Olympic standards. They do not involve loss of face; nor do they demonstrate weakness. In fact they demonstrate the opposite: a sense of sufficient strength and sophistication to understand what is actually taking place in conflict. Threats and the use of violence may well be effective in the short term, but eventually they are more likely to lead to the desire for retaliation and retribution. *Making Terrorism History* calls for something more subtle, slower and painstaking, which requires an attempt to enter into the minds of those who are using political violence – not because violence is in any way condoned, but because violence is the symptom of a much deeper problem that needs addressing.

The power of change in the human heart is formidable. It can transform violent activists into statesmen. The development undergone by Nelson Mandela during his years on Robben Island, after he was convicted of terrorism, made it possible for him to emerge from jail unshakeably committed to negotiation and reconciliation. There were enough people on both sides ready to plunge South Africa into a civil war that could have cost millions of lives; this was averted only because of the depth of his and his colleagues' conviction.

In Iraq and Afghanistan the methods we have described would undoubtedly have taken longer to create regime change, and would have posed plenty of difficulties. But they would have resulted in few civilian or military casualties, little physical destruction, and none of the current bitterness and hatred towards the occupying forces. Non-military support for progress to a multi-party state could eventually have produced an Iraqi opposition capable of government, as has happened in South Africa, the Philippines, Poland, Hungary, Czechoslovakia, East Timor and so on. By enabling a people to decide its own future, rather than imposing military rule, the current level of anger and resentment towards the US and the UK – with all the latent contribution to terrorism – would have been avoided.

Preventing war works on the same principle as inoculation for smallpox – it has to be done methodically, with proven vaccines, and as a fundamental, properly funded policy. Every non-military option should be tested before war is started. Policy-makers need to integrate this into their planning, and understand that the approach currently being advocated by Western governments is simply reinforcing problems rather than finding solutions. Serious planning and serious funding need to be devoted to non-military ways of managing conflict. The UK, for example, currently allocates to conflict prevention and resolution less than half of 1 per cent of the funding allocated for military intervention – and the UK has a better record in this than all except the Scandinavian countries. There is now plentiful evidence that non-military intervention in conflict is cost-effective, and that military intervention can be counter-productive, as became evident for example in Falluja.

The damage done to the fabric of society by any war has to be healed if a lasting peace is to be established. Reconstructing buildings is the easy part. What is most difficult, and least attended to, are the deep wounds left in the minds and hearts of those who live on. Innocent people on all sides will have been killed, women raped, children made mute by the horrors they have witnessed, or left to manage stumps of limbs. Other children are yet to be blown to pieces by unexploded bombs.

If the resulting rage and grief are not addressed they will foment revenge and future terror, and fester into further horror. That's why serious skill and serious money must be invested in this healing. It is why governments must be persuaded that the human factor – human security, rather than the use of force – offers the best chance of making terrorism history.

Notes

1. Personal communication, 16 Feb. 2005.
2. *Falluja*, Study Centre for Democracy and Human Rights report, Jan. 2005.
3. R. Chandrasekaran, 'Key general criticizes April attack in Falluja; abrupt withdrawal called vacillation', *Washington Post*, 13 Sept. 2004.
4. R. Dudai and D. Baram, 'The second battle of Algiers', *Guardian*, 30 Oct. 2004.
5. Ehsan Masood, 'A Muslim Journey', *Prospect*, August 2005.
6. D. A. Macgregor, 'Dramatic failures require drastic changes', *St Louis Post-Dispatch*, 19 Dec. 2004.
7. D. Baum, '67 battle lessons: what the generals don't know', *New Yorker*, 17 Jan. 2005.
8. Telephone communication from Sami Velioglu, 6 July 2004.
9. M. Kaldor, 'The red zone', in R. Belcher (ed.), *Re-imagining Security* (London: British Council, 2004).
10. The Amman Roundtable: Human Security in the Middle East, Amman, Jordan, May 2004, was co-hosted by Prince El Hassan bin Talal with the Oxford Research Group; see www.oxfordresearchgroup.org.uk (accessed 26 June 2005).
11. C. Garland (ed.), *Understanding Trauma: A Psychoanalytical Approach* (London: Duckworth, 2000).
12. Kaldor, 'The red zone'.
13. *Understanding Islamism*, International Crisis Group, Middle East/North Africa Report No. 37, 2 Mar. 2005.
14. A. Crooke and B. Milton-Edwards, 'Should we talk to political Islam?', in Belcher, *Re-imagining Security*.
15. N. J. Chodorow, 'Hate, humiliation and masculinity', in S. Varvin and V. D. Volkan (eds.), *Violence or Dialogue? Psychoanalytic Insights on Terror and Terrorism* (London: International Psychoanalytical Association, 2003).
16. P. Mansfield, *A History of the Middle East*, 2nd edn (London: Penguin, 2003).
17. M. Bunting, 'Honour and martyrdom', *Guardian*, 14 May 2005.
18. C. Conetta, *Vicious Circle: The Dynamics of Occupation and Resistance in Iraq*, Project on Defense Alternatives, Research Monograph No. 10, 18 May 2005.
19. N. Hassan, 'Talking to the human bombs', *New Yorker*, 19 Nov. 2001.

20. Chodorow, 'Hate, humiliation and masculinity'.
21. W. Bohleber, 'Collective phantasms, destructiveness and terrorism', in Varvin and Volkan, *Violence or Dialogue?*
22. Michael Bond, 'The making of a suicide bomber', *New Scientist*, 15 May 2004.
23. Kathleen Taylor, 'Thought crime: brainwashing is routinely invoked to explain atrocities but what does it really mean', *Guardian*, 8 October 2005.
24. S. Varvin, 'Terrorism and victimization', in Varvin and Volkan, *Violence or Dialogue?*
25. V. Kennedy, 'Hope flowers', *Living Lightly*, no. 30, winter 2004.
26. M. Abdulajewa, *Nowaja Gaseta.*
27. Titles on peacekeeping include W. Shawcross, *Deliver Us from Evil: Peacekeepers, Warlords and a World of Endless Conflict* (London: Bloomsbury, 2001); M. Rose, *Fighting for Peace: Bosnia 1994* (London: Harvill, 1998); S. Gordon and F. Toase (eds.), *Aspects of Peacekeeping* (London: Frank Cass, 2001); United Nations General Assembly Security Council, *Report of the Panel on the United Nations Peace Operations*, A/55/305, Aug. 2000.
28. *Cutting the Costs of War: Non-Military Prevention and Resolution of Conflict* (Oxford: Peace Direct and Oxford Research Group, 2004); Department for International Development, *Understanding and Supporting Security Sector Reform* (London: DfID, 2002).
29. Naeemah Abrahams Ph.D., 'Sexual violence against women in South Africa' in *Sexuality in Africa*, vol. 1, issue 3, 2004.
30. Ibid.
31. At the time of writing, Israel had not initiated its withdrawal from Gaza.
32. 'An International Protectorate for Gaza and West Bank', Middle East Policy Initiative Forum, May 2003; available at www.mepif.org (accessed 26 June 2005).
33. Dalai Lama, *Book of Love and Compassion* (London: Thorsons, 2001).
34. Professor Michael Nagler, founder of the University of California Peace and Conflict Studies Program, estimates that nearly one-third of the world's people have practised some form of non-violence, or 'life force', for the redress of grievances. See M. Nagler, *The Search for a Non Violent Future* (Berkeley, Cal.: Berkeley Hills Books, 2001).
35. O. Roy, *Globalised Islam: The Search for a New Ummah* (London: Hurst & Co., 2004).
36. J. Lamb et al., *Wounds of War* (Cambridge, Mass.: Harvard Center for

Population and Development Studies, 2004).

37. 'I Am Prepared to Die': Nelson Mandela's statement before the Rivonia Trial, Pretoria Supreme Court, 20 April 1964.

38. Professor Michael Nagler, *Is There No Other Way: The Search for a Nonviolent Future* (Maui: Inner Ocean Publishing, 2001).

39. J. Burke, 'The Arab backlash the militants did not expect', *Observer*, 20 June 2004.

40. Psychology describes this demonisation as 'projection' – the transferring of our own overwhelming feelings on to others when we feel vulnerable and our survival appears threatened. In a state of vulnerability we feel helpless, powerless and without hope. We split off from the unbearable feelings inside ourselves and project them on to others. The more that victims refuse to accept their own vulnerable part, the more they try to humiliate others and, in the process, deny those others any normal human emotions. They dehumanise the enemy and attribute all kinds of negative qualities to them. It is a process that prevents a richer understanding of other groups and a full engagement with their complexity.

41. D. Matthews, *War Prevention Works* (Oxford: Oxford Research Group, 2001).

42. See the case histories of women in Sierra Leone, Burundi, Colombia and Afghanistan recorded in *Women's World*, no. 37, 2003.

43. An example of a model for intervention for traumatic stress disorders after war, terror or torture would be M. Schauer, F. Neuner and T. Elbert, *Narrative Exposure Therapy* (Cambridge, Mass.: Hogrefe & Huber Publishers, 2005).

44. J. Gittings and I. Davis (eds.), *Re-thinking Defence and Foreign Policy* (Nottingham: Spokesman, 1996).

45. See the following link for discussion of truth commissions: www.lss.org.za/Pubs/Monographs/No68/Chap11.html (accessed 1 July 2005). See also C. Hesse and R. Post (eds.), *Human Rights in Political Transitions: Gettysburg to Bosnia* (New York: Zone Books, 1999).

46. 'A Human Security Doctrine for Europe: The Barcelona Report of the Study Group on Europe's Security Capabilities', presented to the EU High Representative for Common Foreign and Security Policy Javier Solana, 15 September 2004.

47. For more details of Mary Kaldor's work see www.lse.ac.uk/Dept/global (accessed 26 June 2005).

48. The British organisation is Peaceworkers UK; see

www.peaceworkers.org.uk (accessed 26 June 2005).
49. R. Schoch, 'A conversation with Michael Nagler'; see
www.alumni.berkeley.edu/Alumni/Cal_Monthly/December_2001/
QA-_A_conversation_with_Michael_Nagler.asp (accessed 1 July 2005).
50. Conetta, *Vicious Circle*.
51. J. Gillian-Borg (ed.), *SIPRI Yearbook 2002: Armaments, Disarmament
and International Security* (Oxford: Oxford University Press, 2002).
52. *Human Security Now* (New York: The Commission on
Human Security, 2003).
53. Lamb et al., *Wounds of War*.
54. See, among others, P. Ingram and I. Davis, *The Subsidy Trap: British
Government Financial Support for Arms Export* (Oxford: Saferworld
and Oxford Research Group, 2001).
55. Personal communication from Dr Mo Mowlam, 11 May 2004.